BOMB-SNIFFING DOGS

by Meish Goldish

Consultant: Freddie R. Brasfield
K-9 Search on Site

BEARPORT
PUBLISHING

New York, New York

Credits

Cover and Title Page, © Michael Ventura/Alamy; Cover TR, © Mark Avery/ZUMA Press/Newscom; Cover CR, © AP Photo/Alan Diaz; Cover BR, © Mandi Wright/KRT/Newscom; TOC, © Mandi Wright/KRT/Newscom; 4, © Romeo Gacad/AFP/Getty Images; 5, © Press Association via AP Images; 6, © Patrick Baz/AFP/Getty Images; 7, © U.S. Army; 8, © U.S. Army/Lance Cpl. Andrew Young/Reuters/Newscom; 9, © Jeff Topping/Reuters/Landov; 10, © Mark Avery/ZUMA Press/Newscom; 11, © AP Photo/Alan Diaz; 12, © Mandi Wright/KRT/Newscom; 13, © Jim Gehrz/Star Tribune/Newscom; 14, © U.S. Air Force/Robbin Cresswell; 15L, © AP Photo/Eric Gay; 15R, © Michael Ventura/Alamy; 16, © U.S. Air Force/Airman 1st Class Anthony Sanchelli; 17L, © Marka/SuperStock; 17R, © Marka/SuperStock; 18, © AP Photo/Alan Diaz; 19, © Chuck Crow/The Plain Dealer/Landov; 20T, © 2010, The Oklahoma Publishing Company; 20B, © Marka/SuperStock; 21, © U.S. DOD/Cpl. Tom Sloan; 22, © U.S. Air Force; 22–23, © Xinhua/Iqbal Hussain/Newscom; 24, © Auburn University Collection; 25, © Brendan Smialowski/Getty Images; 26, © AP Photo/Idaho Statesman/Joe Jaszewski; 27, © AP Photo/Gregory Bull; 28, © Namir Noor-Eldeen/Reuters/Newscom; 29TL, © Eric Isselée/Shutterstock; 29TR, © Erik Lam/Shutterstock; 29BL, © Eric Isselée/Shutterstock; 29BR, © Exactostock/SuperStock.

Publisher: Kenn Goin
Editorial Director: Adam Siegel
Creative Director: Spencer Brinker
Design: Dawn Beard Creative
Photo Researcher: Picture Perfect Professionals, LLC

Library of Congress Cataloging-in-Publication Data

Goldish, Meish.
  Bomb-sniffing dogs / by Meish Goldish.
    p. cm. — (Dog heroes)
  "K-9 search on site."
  Includes bibliographical references and index.
  ISBN-13: 978-1-61772-455-8 (library binding)
  ISBN-10: 1-61772-455-6 (library binding)
 1. Police dogs—Juvenile literature. 2. Search dogs—Juvenile literature. 3. Detector dogs—Juvenile literature. I. Title.
  HV8025.G65 2012
  363.325'163—dc23

                    2011038302

For more information, write to Bearport Publishing Company, Inc., 45 West 21st Street, Suite 3B, New York, New York 10010. Printed in the United States of America in North Mankato, Minnesota.

10 9 8 7 6 5 4 3 2 1

Table of Contents

Hidden Dangers

In March 2010, British soldiers in Afghanistan were on **patrol** with a Belgian shepherd named Chocolat. They came to a row of empty shops. Suddenly, the dog walked ahead of the men. He entered one of the stores by himself. Normally, Chocolat would never have left the sight of his **handler**, Private Steve Purdy. When the dog wouldn't come out of the building, Private Purdy knew that Chocolat must have smelled something dangerous inside.

The type of Belgian shepherd dog used to sniff for bombs is called a Malinois (mal-uhn-WAH).

Dasty, a Belgian Malinois, patrols a village in Afghanistan.

Soldiers carefully entered the shop. They discovered a huge supply of **explosives** hidden by the enemy. There were enough materials to make more than ten powerful bombs. Thanks to Chocolat, the weapons had been found before they could do any harm. Yet the soldiers now wondered: Were more bombs hidden nearby?

This British soldier and his dog are searching for bombs in Afghanistan.

A Deadly Trap

The soldiers continued to patrol the street. They soon spotted a large homemade bomb in front of another shop. A bomb expert was told to **defuse** it. He was **suspicious**, however. The **device** had been found too easily. He feared it might be wired to other bombs hidden nearby. Were the soldiers being led into a deadly trap?

Soldiers and their bomb-sniffing dog patrol the streets in Afghanistan.

Private Purdy sent Chocolat to sniff out a safe path to the back of the building. After following the bomb-sniffing dog, the soldiers blew open a hole in the back wall. Once inside the building, they could see that many other bombs were hidden in the area around the store. By safely leading the soldiers to the back of the building, Chocolat had once again helped save their lives.

Homemade bombs used to attack an enemy, such as these, are called improvised explosive devices, or IEDs.

Improvised explosive devices are also called roadside bombs.

On the Job

Chocolat is one of thousands of dogs trained to **detect** explosives. Some of these bomb sniffers, including Chocolat, serve in the **military**. They assist soldiers in war zones. Using their sharp sense of smell, the dogs find bombs the enemy has hidden in buildings or on the side of the road to harm **troops**.

U.S. soldiers and their bomb-sniffing dog climb up to the roof of a building in Iraq to search for explosives.

Soldiers are not the only people, however, who work with bomb-sniffing dogs. Police use them to patrol busy travel areas such as airports and bus stations. They're also on duty in crowded public places like malls and sports stadiums. Some private companies even hire the dogs to protect their offices and workers.

Sandman, a yellow Labrador retriever, checks for bombs at the University of Phoenix Stadium in Arizona.

Dogs are good bomb sniffers because they have a strong sense of smell and can move quickly. As a result, it is easy for them to check out a large area in very little time.

9

An Early Hero

Because **terrorists** often try to use explosives to threaten people, bringing in bomb-sniffing dogs is a good way to stop them. One of the first dogs trained to find bombs was a German shepherd named Brandy. On March 9, 1972, she got a surprise chance to prove her skills. On that day, Trans World Airlines (TWA) received a phone call warning that a bomb had been placed on a plane flying from New York to Los Angeles. The plane, which had just taken off from New York, quickly returned to the airport.

A German shepherd, similar to the one here, was one of the first bomb-sniffing dogs.

Amazingly, Brandy happened to be at the airport. She had been brought there to demonstrate her bomb-sniffing skills. As soon as the passengers got off the plane, the police brought Brandy on board to sniff around. The dog led them to a briefcase in the **cockpit**. Police were shocked to find a bomb inside. They defused it just 12 minutes before it was set to explode!

In the early 1970s, scientists began to study dogs to see if they could use their sense of smell to locate bombs. Brandy was one of the dogs in this training program.

Andorra, a member of the Miami-Dade Police Department, is one of many bomb-sniffing dogs that now work at airports across the United States.

Top Dogs

Brandy did her job well. However, not all dogs make good bomb sniffers. Four **breeds** are considered the best for this job. They are German shepherds, Belgian Malinois, Labrador retrievers, and vizslas (VEEZH-luhz). All are **ideal** bomb sniffers because they have an especially keen sense of smell. They also stay calm in crowds and around strangers.

Because Labrador retrievers work well around people, they are often used to search crowded areas such as airports and malls.

A Labrador retriever named Marla checks the luggage at Metro Airport in Romulus, Michigan.

Of all bomb-sniffing dogs, German shepherds are the most popular. The dogs smell extremely well because their noses have about 220 million sniffing **cells**. By comparison, a human has only about 5 million sniffing cells. In addition, German shepherds are smart, **loyal**, and easy to train. They also react quickly to danger.

Radar is a bomb-sniffing dog that works on the Hiawatha Light Rail in Minneapolis, Minnesota.

Teaming Up

Bomb sniffing isn't something dogs know how to do when they are born. They must be taught the skill. Dogs that work for the U.S. military are taught how to find bombs at Lackland Air Force Base in San Antonio, Texas. The dogs spend about 11 weeks there. During that time, the dogs are also taught basic **obedience** skills, such as sitting and staying.

Valerie is learning basic obedience commands at Lackland Air Force Base.

Dogs that will be trained to detect bombs come from many sources, including Lackland Air Force Base's own breeding program, professional breeders, shelters, and families.

While at Lackland, each dog is paired with a handler who trains, feeds, and **grooms** the animal. Over time, the handler gets to know his or her dog's behavior and habits. The dog even lives with the handler. By spending lots of time together, the two are able to **bond**. After training is completed, the handler will work with the dog on the job.

Bomb-sniffing dogs, such as this Labrador retriever, usually are trained when they are between one and three years old. That's when they are most willing to learn.

John Long, a handler, and his dog, Coby, train together at Lackland Air Force Base.

The Nose Knows

As part of their training, bomb-sniffing dogs must learn to identify the smell of explosives. Bombs may contain a mix of different chemicals, plus other materials, such as **fertilizer**. Each material has a specific odor, or **scent**. Every day, the handler works with his or her dog to help the **canine** learn to recognize one individual scent.

Bomb-sniffing dogs are able to smell explosives even if they are hidden in a container with something else that has a different odor, such as a bottle of perfume or a jar of peanut butter.

The handler starts by giving the dog an item such as a tube with small holes in it. Material used to make a bomb is placed inside the tube. The dog smells the scent through the holes. Each time the dog smells the material, the animal gets a reward. After two or three days, the dog has learned to recognize and remember the scent. The handler then starts hiding scented items for the dog to find.

This dog has found a box containing explosive materials.

A handler placing a scented tube into a box for a dog to find

By the end of its training, a bomb-sniffing dog has learned to recognize 12 to 20 explosive scents.

17

"I Found It!"

Once a dog detects the scent of a bomb, it must let its handler know immediately. Usually, the canine is taught to sit quietly and face the direction of the smell it has found. When the dog sits, the handler knows an explosive is nearby.

This dog sat down to let its handler know that it had found an explosive inside a car.

Dogs are trained to search for bombs hidden in objects such as boxes, suitcases, and cars.

Not all dogs are taught to sit when they find a bomb. Some dogs are taught to bark or point their noses toward the scent. Others may wag their tails or scratch the ground with their paws. All dogs are taught, however, never to touch the explosive. In a real-life search, touching the bomb might set it off and injure or kill everyone nearby.

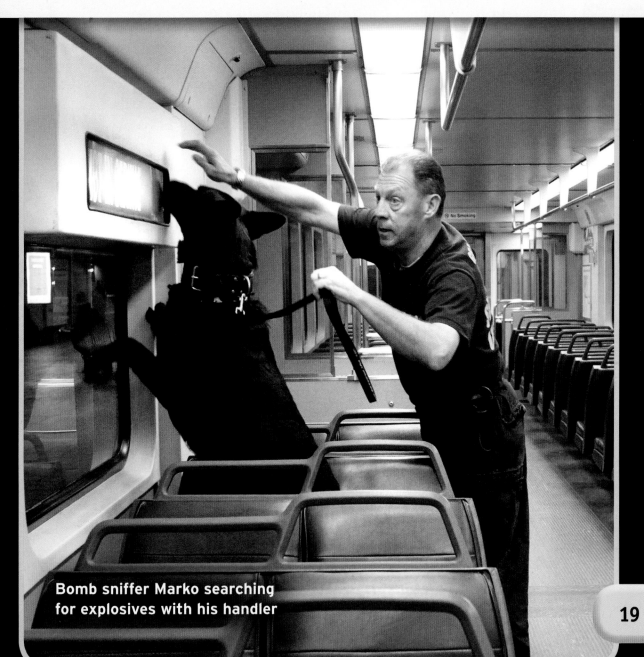

Bomb sniffer Marko searching for explosives with his handler

Play and Rewards

Detecting bombs is deadly serious work. Yet to the dog, it's all just a playful game of hide-and-seek. After the animal finds the hidden item, it signals its handler and waits to be rewarded. The handler gives the animal lots of hugs and praise each time it succeeds in finding a bomb.

Brian Nelson's dog, Ambra, thinks of a bomb search as a game.

Because people sometimes hide bombs in hard-to-reach places, bomb-sniffing dogs are often trained to climb ladders and jump through **obstacles**.

Handlers offer their dogs other kinds of rewards as well. Often they give the canines a rubber ball or some other toy to play with. While some handlers use food as a reward, most find that the dogs enjoy toys much more.

Rex, a Belgian Malinois, likes to play ball with his handler.

Having Trust

Handlers trust their bomb-sniffing partners with their lives. Just ask Staff Sergeant Joseph Null. In 2009, he and his dog, Lucca, were given a dangerous assignment in Iraq. They were ordered to check for bombs that the enemy might have planted near an army supply truck loaded with 22,000 gallons (83,279 l) of gasoline. The truck had gotten stuck in the sand, so it had been **abandoned**.

Staff Sergeant Joseph Null poses with Lucca. "If you can't trust the dog, you shouldn't be out there," he said.

Lucca and Staff Sergeant Null searched the area around the truck for 45 minutes. The soldier put all his trust in his dog. If a bomb exploded, the gasoline would create a huge and deadly explosion. Luckily, Lucca never sat down. He found no bombs in the area. Eight hours later the truck was safely pulled out of the sand.

Arctic Ocean

ASIA

NORTH AMERICA

EUROPE   Iraq Afghanistan

Atlantic Ocean

AFRICA

Pacific Ocean

Pacific Ocean

SOUTH AMERICA

Indian Ocean

AUSTRALIA

N
W   E
S

Southern Ocean

In 2011, about 170 bomb-sniffing dogs served alongside the U.S. **Marines** in Afghanistan and Iraq.

A gasoline truck can become a powerful bomb if it catches fire and explodes.

New and Improved

In recent years, bomb-sniffing dogs have gotten even better at their jobs. They've always been able to smell an explosive that is nearby and not moving. Now new **vapor-wake detection** (VWD) dogs can track down a bomb on a person walking through a large area such as an airport or a mall. How do they do it?

A handler at Auburn University trains VWD dogs.

Research on vapor-wake detection began at Auburn University in Alabama in 2004.

VWD dogs don't just smell the scent coming from a nearby bomb. They're trained to smell the air that swirls behind people as they walk. Items leave a trail of odors behind them as they travel. If someone walks with a bomb, a VWD dog can track the vapor trail coming from the bomb even 15 minutes after the person has left the area!

Zeta, a vapor-wake detection dog, works at a train station in Washington, D.C.

After Work

How long does a bomb sniffer's career last? It depends. Some dogs are injured on the job. If the injuries are too serious for a full recovery, the dogs are forced to stop working. On average, however, a bomb-sniffing dog works about seven to nine years before it retires.

Yuma worked as a bomb sniffer for eight years with the police department in Boise, Idaho, before retiring in 2011 at the age of 11.

Police officers often keep their bomb-sniffing dogs as pets when they retire. In the past, however, U.S. law required that all retired military bomb-sniffing dogs be put to sleep. Then a law was passed in 2000 that allowed people to adopt the dogs. Many retired military bomb sniffers now happily live out their lives with their handlers' families. It's a fitting reward for those canines that have served faithfully to help make the world a safer place.

Chyba is a retired military dog that served in Iraq.

Retired military bomb-sniffing dogs used to be put to sleep, because it was believed the war dogs were too **aggressive** and hard to handle to become household pets.

Just the Facts

- The same day Brandy discovered a bomb on a TWA flight in 1972, President Richard Nixon ordered that programs be created to keep airports safe from explosives. The result was that bomb-sniffing dogs were placed at major U.S. airports.

- Amtrak began using vapor-wake detection dogs on their trains and in railway stations in 2008. In 2011, vapor-wake detection dogs were brought in to help out at Los Angeles International Airport.

- Without the help of dogs, American soldiers in Iraq and Afghanistan can find about 50 percent of the improvised explosive devices hidden by the enemy. However, when bomb-sniffing dogs patrol with the soldiers, the teams find about 80 percent of the devices.

A U.S. soldier stands guard with a bomb-sniffing dog in Iraq.

German shepherd

Belgian Malinois

Labrador retriever

vizsla

abandoned (uh-BAN-duhnd) left alone and uncared for; deserted

aggressive (uh-GRESS-iv) acting in a forceful or threatening way

bond (BOND) to develop a close friendship or connection

breeds (BREEDZ) kinds of dogs

canine (KAY-nine) a member of the dog family

cells (SELZ) basic, very tiny parts of a person, animal, or plant

cockpit (KOK-pit) the area in the front of a plane where the pilot sits and flies the plane

defuse (dee-FYOOZ) to take apart a bomb to prevent it from exploding

detect (di-TEKT) to notice or discover something

device (di-VYESS) a piece of equipment that does a particular job

explosives (ek-SPLOH-sivz) substances that can blow up things

fertilizer (FUR-tuh-*lye*-zur) a substance added to soil to make plants grow better

grooms (GROOMZ) brushes and cleans

handler (HAND-lur) a person who trains and works with an animal

ideal (eye-DEE-uhl) perfect

loyal (LOI-uhl) faithful to others

Marines (muh-REENZ) a branch of the U.S. military; Marines are trained to fight on land, at sea, and in the air

military (MIL-uh-*ter*-ee) the armed forces of a country

obedience (oh-BEE-dee-uhnss) the act of doing what one is told to do

obstacles (OB-stuh-kuhlz) things that block a path

patrol (puh-TROHL) walking or traveling around an area to protect it

scent (SENT) a smell or odor

suspicious (suh-SPISH-uhss) having questions or doubts

terrorists (TER-ur-ists) people or groups that use violence and terror to get what they want

troops (TROOPS) groups of soldiers

vapor-wake detection (VAY-pur-WAYK di-TEK-shuhn) smelling the air for odors that an object leaves behind as it travels

Bibliography

Hamer, Blythe. *Dogs at War: True Stories of Canine Courage Under Fire.* London: Carlton (2006).

Kaldenbach, Jan. *K9 Scent Detection.* Calgary, Canada: Detselig Enterprises (1998).

Mistafa, Ron. *K9 Explosive Detection.* Calgary, Canada: Detselig Enterprises (1998).

Rogak, Lisa. *The Dogs of War: The Courage, Love, and Loyalty of Military Working Dogs.* New York: St. Martin's Griffin (2011).

Read More

Goldish, Meish. *War Dogs (America's Animal Soldiers).* New York: Bearport (2012).

Grayson, Robert. *Military (Working Animals).* Tarrytown, NY: Marshall Cavendish Benchmark (2011).

Osborne, Mary Pope, and Natalie Pope Boyce. *Dog Heroes.* New York: Random House (2011).

Ruffin, Frances E. *Military Dogs (Dog Heroes).* New York: Bearport (2007).

Learn More Online

Visit these Web sites to learn more about bomb-sniffing dogs:

http://landofpuregold.com/explosives-sproul.htm

www.tsa.gov/lawenforcement/programs/editorial_multi_image_0002.shtm

www.tsa.gov/lawenforcement/programs/puppy_program.shtm

www.vetmed.auburn.edu/vapor-wake-detection

Index

About the Author

Meish Goldish has written more than 200 books for children. His book *Heart-Stopping Roller Coasters* was a Children's Choices Selection in 2011. He lives in Brooklyn, New York.